Wild animals

Les animaux sauvages

lezanee*mo* so-*vajsh*

Illustrated by Clare Beaton

Illustré par Clare Beaton

BARRON'S

hippopotamus

l'hippopotame

leepo-po*tam*

elephant

l'éléphant

lellay-foh

lion

le lion

leh lee-*oh*

polar bear

l'ours blanc

loo-rss bloh

tiger

le tigre

leh teegr'

monkey

le singe

leh sanjsh

zebra

le zèbre

leh zaibr'

crocodile

le crocodile

leh croco*deel*

kangaroo

le kangourou

leh kongoo-*roo*

giraffe

la girafe

lah sheeraff

snake

le serpent

leh sair-*poh*

A simple guide to pronouncing the French words★

- Read this guide as naturally as possible, as if it were English.
- Put stress on the letters in *italics* e.g. leh sair-*poh*.
- Remember that the final consonants in French generally are silent.

l'hippopotame	leepo-po*tam*	**hippopotamus**
l'éléphant	lellay-*foh*	**elephant**
le lion	leh lee-*oh*	**lion**
l'ours blanc	loo-rss bloh	**polar bear**
le tigre	leh teegr'	**tiger**
le singe	leh sanjsh	**monkey**
le zèbre	leh zaibr'	**zebra**
le crocodile	leh croco*deel*	**crocodile**
le kangourou	leh kongoo-*roo*	**kangaroo**
la girafe	lah shee*raff*	**giraffe**
le serpent	leh sair-*poh*	**snake**

★There are many different guides to pronunciation. Our guide attempts to balance precision with simplicity.